THE ‹
Unlocking the

Jeremy Mahurin

The Secret Place: Unlocking the Power of the Presence of God
Copyright ©2009 Rev. Jeremy Mahurin

Visit our website: www.drawingcloser.org

Request for information should be addressed to:

> Rev. Jeremy Mahurin
> 15360 Hwy C   Dixon, MO 65459
> 573-759-3192

> Mahurin, Jeremy
> The Secret Place / Jeremy Mahurin
> ISBN-13: 978-0-9824393-0-2
> ISBN-10: 0-9824393-0-X
> 1. Christian Life. 2. Prayer. I. Title.

All scripture quotations, unless otherwise indicated, are taken from the New King James Version®. Copyright © 1982 by Thomas Nelson, Inc. Used by permission. All rights reserved.

Scripture quotations marked (NIV) are taken from the HOLY BIBLE, NEW INTERNATIONAL VERSION®. NIV®. Copyright© 1973, 1978, 1984 by International Bible Society. Used by permission of Zondervan. All rights reserved.

All rights reserved. No part of this publication may be reproduced; whether electronically, mechanically, photocopied, recorded or any other means, except for brief quotations in printed reviews, without the prior permission of the author.

Book cover design and text formatting by: Charity Mahurin
   For more information: (573)528-4347

Printed in the United States of America
Diamond Publishing   Mobile, AL

DEDICATION

I would like to dedicate this book to the heritage that was passed down to me by my parents and grandparents. Both of my grandfathers were pastors, and my grandmothers were dedicated pastor's wives. They showed their children what it meant to know God. Because of their diligence, I have five uncles who are in the ministry. Their passion for knowing God was also passed down to my father and mother.

My parents instilled in me the importance of a relationship with God from an early age. They were the epitome of the charge in the Bible to train a child in the way they should go. My parents raised three children; all of us are currently in the ministry.

In this life, they will never be properly recognized for their work. However, I know that none of their diligence has gone unnoticed in Heaven. Mom and Dad, you don't get enough credit for the job that you did, but countless lives have been changed in your ministry and countless more will continue to be changed as a result of the heritage you passed on to your children. I hope my children see in me the same example I saw in you. Thank you for who you are and the path you have shown me to follow.

TABLE OF CONTENTS

Introduction..7

The Holy Spirit Changes Us in the Secret Place......9

Jesus Christ in the Secret Place...........................12

What the Secret Place is Not...............................16

Defining the Secret Place....................................22

What to Do in the Secret Place............................37

What to Keep in the Secret Place........................44

Benefits of the Secret Place................................48

You Can Know Him!...74

INTRODUCTION

I would like to begin this book with a simple question: *"Are you as close to God as you want to be?"* It may be a simple question, but answering it honestly can bring great changes in your life. Do you know God's voice? Do you feel His joy? Do you feel His pain? The realization that I was not as close to God as I would like to have been was the inspiration for writing this book.

Even as a minister of the gospel, I did not have the intimate relationship with God that He desired to have with me. He wanted a closer relationship with me. He wanted us to spend time together, so I could get to know Him better and learn all the intricacies of His personality.

I had a relationship with God where I talked to Him but did not give Him the opportunity to reveal Himself to me. I mostly talked to God on the run. It was like having a conversation with someone on a cell phone while driving in traffic. It is better than not speaking at all, but it is difficult to have a very deep conversation because of all of the distractions. I wanted something better in my walk with God, so I began looking for answers.

I asked God to show me the secret to having a more intimate, personal relationship with Him. I wanted to have conversations with God like He was my best friend, not just the great, celestial being that He is. I wanted to know Him, not just His power. I wanted to know Him, not just His grace. I wanted to know Him, not just His blessings. I wanted to know what He likes, what He dislikes, what He enjoys and what He despises. I wanted to get past the religious ceremony and trying to impress God with flowery prayers—I wanted to know HIM.

There was something missing in my relationship with God. I heard one of my mentors, Dr. Mike Brown, talking a lot about the secret place. I began pondering the subject of the secret place. How is it different than a normal prayer life? How is it any different from normal devotions with God? I began praying about that subject.

While attending a minister's conference I spent time in the hotel room alone with God asking Him to reveal the secret place to me. The next hour was one of the greatest times of communion with God that I have ever experienced. I felt as though the Holy Spirit was sitting beside me in that hotel room personally mentoring me on the art of sitting in the presence of God. This book is the product of that awe-inspiring encounter with God.

THE HOLY SPIRIT CHANGES US IN THE SECRET PLACE

God first revealed to me that the secret place was the place where the Holy Spirit can change us. In one of the sessions at the minister's conference I was attending, Dr. Mike Brown made the following statement: "The Holy Spirit is obsessed with causing us to BE something, not causing us to DO something." The Holy Spirit wants to change who we are. He wants to change our nature.

Acts 1:8 says, *"But you shall receive power when the Holy Spirit has come upon you; and you shall __BE__ witnesses to Me"*. Jesus says that we will BE witnesses, not do witnessing things. He wants to make us BE something, not make us do something. If we will allow the Holy Spirit to cause us to be who He wants us to be, we will automatically do what He wants us to do. As Christians we spend a lot of time trying to do Christian things. God does not want us to merely be doing Christian things; He wants us to be like Christ. If we will learn to walk in an intimate relationship with the Holy Spirit, He will not have to cause us to do daily

> "The Holy Spirit is obsessed with causing us to BE something, not causing us to DO something."
> Dr. Mike Brown

devotionals—we will long for the opportunity to spend time each day with God because we love spending time with Him. He will not have to force us to do witnessing things—we will share the good news of the gospel with others because of the excitement in our heart generated by experiencing His presence.

"Being" does not come from "doing". "Doing" comes from "being". In other words, we are not who we are because of what we do, rather we do what we do because of who we are. Many people are trying to do Christian things when they simply have not been changed by the Holy Spirit. As I have heard said, "An apple tree doesn't have a nervous breakdown trying to grow apples." If we become who God wants us to be, we will not struggle to bear the fruit we need to bear. It will come natural because it is what we were created to do. In order to be a kingdom achiever and accomplish what God has in store, we must be molded into what the Holy Spirit wants us to be.

The question is, *"How do we allow the Holy Spirit access to change our hearts?"* The answer is to meet Him in the secret place where He is able to show us things in our lives that need changed or improved. Without meeting God in the secret place we can never reach the highest heights that God has made available to us. God cannot change us into the best possible person we can be without the access that the secret place brings.

The following chapters are designed to guide you in your quest to meet God in the secret place and allow Him to reveal Himself to you and change you into the person that He wants you to be.

JESUS CHRIST IN THE SECRET PLACE

You may be asking, *"Why is it important for me to have a secret place?"* The simplest answer I can give is that Jesus Christ thought it was extremely important to get away from everyone in order to spend time with God the Father. There are many examples of Jesus Christ drawing away from the crowds to have a time of private devotion.

> *Now in the morning, having risen*
> *a long while before daylight,*
> *He (Jesus) went out and departed*
> *to a solitary place; and there He prayed.*
> Mark 1:35 NKJV

Mark 1:35 gives an example of Jesus going to a solitary place to pray early in the morning. I believe this is one of the keys to walking with God. It is vitally important that we commune with God in the morning in order to start our day off with the correct focus. We will discuss this further in a later chapter.

> *Immediately He made His disciples get into the boat and go before Him to the other side, to Bethsaida, while He sent the multitude away. And when He had sent them away, He departed to the mountain to pray. Now when*

evening came, the boat was in the middle of the sea; and He was alone on the land.
Mark 6:45-48 NKJV

This is the beginning of the very well-known story of Jesus walking on the water. Here, we see Jesus making His disciples leave so He could go to the secret place to pray. The disciples left Him as they set sail. After He had His time with God the Father, He set out to join them. He walked out on the water to get in the boat with them. Jesus thought spending time alone with God the Father was important enough that He stayed behind as the disciples sailed across the sea. Being with His Heavenly Father was such a priority, He knew that He could not afford to miss it even if it meant relying on a miracle to catch up with the others. His decision to make spending time in the secret place the top priority of His life resulted in one of the greatest stories ever told.

Yet the news about him spread all the more, so that crowds of people came to hear him and to be healed of their sicknesses. But Jesus often withdrew to lonely places and prayed.
Luke 5:15-16 NIV

This passage shows us an example of Jesus' need to be refueled after giving so much of Himself to the people. He had preached to them and healed their sick. After this ministry, Christ needed to withdraw and spend time in the secret place in order to recharge His battery. This is a tremendous example for those in ministry. If we give and give and never receive anything from God, it will not be long before we have nothing left to give. It can easily result in burning out. Jesus understood the importance of receiving from God so that He would have something to offer the people. We also need to heed the importance of this principle.

Now it came to pass in those days that He (Jesus) went out to the mountain to pray, and continued all night in prayer to God.
Luke 6:12 NKJV

    This Biblical example of when the secret place is to be used, shows Jesus Christ praying all night in the secret place because He had a big decision that needed to be made. In the following verse, we see that when day came, He gathered His disciples and named 12 of them apostles. We see how Jesus prepared Himself for making big decisions. We need to follow His example by spending time in our secret place before we make decisions, both spiritual and business. Jesus did not just "wing it"; He took time alone in prayer before He made this announcement. God the Father was His greatest mentor, just as He should be for us.

    This chapter has shown four examples of Jesus Christ spending time in the secret place.

There were various reasons for this time of devotion, but one thing is consistent—He always found time to be alone to pray. No matter the external pressures, no matter the hectic schedules, no matter if the twelve set sail without Him—He placed a high priority on spending time with God the Father. Although He was 100% God, He was also 100% man and saw His own need for daily devotions, refueling and Godly mentoring. If Jesus needed to spend this time alone in prayer, how much more do we need to spend time in the secret place? If the King of Kings and the Lord of Lords needed to recharge His battery after ministering, how much more important is it for us to receive from God in the secret place after we have given of ourselves? We must follow Jesus' example and find every opportunity to spend time alone with our Heavenly Father.

WHAT THE SECRET PLACE IS NOT

*B*efore I begin to tell you what the secret place is, I would like to give some examples of what it is not. I believe that many people do not spend time alone with God in the secret place because they think that their existing prayer life is sufficient. They use some of the following as the foundation for their time with God.

Prayer Before Meals

I doubt that many people who are serious about spending time in the secret place pray only before meals. However, I also think it would be embarrassing for us to count the number of days where the majority of our time spent in prayer for the day is done at the dinner table.

Praying While Driving

I must be honest, I have cried out to Heaven many times while driving. My father is always quick to point out, "Watch and pray" when talking about praying while driving. While I am not opposed to praying from the driver's seat, it is not the best option for being able to have deep conversations with God. There are too many distractions for it to be very effective.

Listening to Worship Music

God greatly appreciates our worship. However, simply popping in a worship CD on your way to work does not mean that you are spending time in the secret place. In order to develop an intimate relationship with God, we must have deep conversations with Him.

Praying At Church

Praying corporate prayers at church is a wonderful thing. Having great altar experiences is an integral part of our walk with God. However, we must talk to God outside the four walls of our church building in order to walk in intimacy with God.

Multitasking Prayers

This category of prayers probably defined a majority of my prayers before I found the secret place. I would pray at work. I would pray while getting ready in the mornings. I would pray while I was trying to go to sleep. I would always pray while I was doing something else. I was able to communicate my needs to God, but was never able to allow

Him to communicate with me. I was always distracted while I prayed.

I have spoken with many great Christians and have come to the conclusion that many Christians pray in this mode more than any other. The major problem with this sort of prayer is that it does not allow God to reveal Himself to us. It is very difficult for God to change us by the power of His Holy Spirit when our conversations are dominated by our supplications.

Some Christians would say, "I pray without ceasing. I am always praying." I would find that incredibly hard to believe. Most people use that as an excuse to not have a scheduled time of prayer, so they do not have to interrupt their busy schedule.

I am not saying that we should never pray while attempting other tasks, but our prayer life should not be made up primarily of this type of prayer.

911 Prayers

In our lives, we will inevitably have emergencies arise and will immediately petition God for an answer. God most certainly does not mind our 911 prayers. In fact, I believe that He loves the opportunity to "show off" His power in these circumstances. However, this is not to be our main source of contact with God.

Casual Prayer Life

I have heard preachers talk many times about spending time with God in the secret place. I always passed it off as some type of flowery, evangelist-speak for having a prayer life. I remember listening to them and thinking, "Yeah, I have a secret place." I did have a prayer life. I just did not have a purposeful prayer life. I prayed when I had time or needed something, but rarely just spent time with God in order to know Him more.

Many Christians miss the power of the Secret Place because they mistakenly think their prayer life needs no work.

I believe many Christians miss the power of the secret place because they mistakenly think their prayer life needs no work. They spend time in prayer several days per week. It may only be for a few minutes one day and a couple another, but they do spend time in prayer.

Do not misunderstand what I am saying. I am not opposed to the types of prayers I have talked about in this chapter; I think anytime we talk to God that it is a good thing. However, there is something better. God has something more available for us if we will meet Him in the secret place. We should not be willing to settle for good, when great is readily available.

I am a general contractor in residential building. When I first started in construction, I did not have an abundance of money. I needed a lot of tools to get started, so I bought several generic brand power tools. I was able to get the job completed with these tools and thought they worked great. Then, my uncle came and worked with me for a few days. He brought DeWalt, Milwaukee and Makita tools to work with. He let me use them while he was there working with me. As I began to use his more expensive tools, I realized that my generic tools were lacking in comparison to his higher quality tools. I was able to get the job done with my tools, but the job was so much easier with his more powerful tools.

I think that our prayer life is much like the difference in those tools. We can get by on a casual, "pray when I have the time" prayer life; but there is so much more power to be found in the secret place that makes everyday living much easier. I was unable to afford the more expensive tools; therefore, I was forced to settle with less than the best for a

> *Something Better is readily available.*
> *We do not need to settle for good enough anymore.*

time. However, the same is not true in our prayer life. The only thing we must do to move from good to great is make ourselves available to God, allow Him to reveal Himself to us, and allow the Holy Spirit to change us. Something better is readily available, and we do not need to settle for good enough anymore.

In the following chapters, I will define the secret place and show you how to apply it in your everyday life. As we discover the secret place, God will be able to more effectively change us and make us more powerful Christians.

DEFINING THE SECRET PLACE

We have discussed the importance that Jesus placed on the secret place and what the secret place is not. Now, we will move on to defining the secret place.

There are five important factors that make the secret place different from a casual prayer life.

The secret place....

- Is a Private Place
- Is a Designated Place
- Is a Scheduled Appointment with God
- Facilitates Mutual Communication
- Allows God to Make You Who He Created You to Be

A Private Place

The secret place is to be a private place where we can be alone with God. Many Biblical examples show God calling men away from the crowds into a private place where He could have special communion with them. He called Moses up to the top of Mount Sinai away from the Israelites to deliver the

Ten Commandments. Jesus went away from the disciples into the Garden of Gethsemane to pray that the cup of the crucifixion would be passed from Him. John wrote the book of Revelation in the solitude of the Isle of Patmos. There are many instances which show that God is able to more clearly speak to us away from the distractions of everyday life.

It is extremely important to go to a private place, where God is your only audience. There, you are able to bare your soul and clearly hear the instructions of the Holy Spirit. When we attempt to pray with distractions, whether it is a phone, television, spouse or children, we are never able to fully enter the presence of God. We must find a place where we are alone with Him, in the shelter of His arms. Anything less does not allow us to completely open up to God and attentively listen to His voice.

The Secret Place is to be a private place where we can be alone with God.

Imagine if you tried to conduct a highly important business meeting with a valued client while a television was on, the telephone was ringing, and your co-workers were running in and out of the meeting room. It would make conducting business nearly impossible. When we are in our secret place, we have the audience of the Creator of the world. What guest could possibly be more important?

The main goal of spending time in the secret place is to gain intimacy with God. There is no other way to have an intimate relationship with God other than spending time alone with Him. Intimacy with God will not come from a great altar experience. It may be birthed there, but it will not grow there. Intimacy with God will not come from talking about God. Talking about Him may create a desire to pursue Him, but it does not bring intimacy with God. We can only find an intimate relationship with God by spending time alone with Him.

A Designated Place

People seem to have a place for everything. If you look at our homes you will see that we have a room where we cook; we have a room where we eat; we have a room where we sleep. At our workplace we have a room where we do our work and a room where we meet. People tend to compartmentalize everything. We have designated a place to do nearly everything in our lives. If it is important for us to have a special place to fix our hair, how much more important is it for us to designate a place to spend time with God.

I believe it is important to have a specific place to meet with God each day. Certainly, the presence of the Holy Spirit is always with us; however, there is power in having a place "set aside" for God. God is a respecter of honor. We display great honor to God when we demonstrate our esteem for Him by setting aside a place in our home where we go only to meet with Him.

Having a specific place set aside to meet God only fosters a special bond between us and God. It creates a climate that produces intimacy. When we go to that place, we know exactly what we are there to do. God knows exactly why we are there. It makes it easy to enter into the presence of God because that is the only thing for which that space is used.

Doctors have told patients with insomnia to be careful to use their bedroom for sleeping only. By using their bedrooms specifically for sleeping, their brain and body know immediately when they go into that room that it is time for sleeping. That room becomes only a room for sleeping, and it becomes automatic for them to go to sleep when they enter that room.

The same can be done in our secret place. If we have a place that is only used for entering the presence of God, our mind realizes that is the place where we meet God. This is the place where the amazing happens: my faith is built, my hope is restored, my body is healed, and my mind is renewed. As soon as you enter that room your expectation begins to soar as your mind remembers what has happened there in the past. You learn to enter there with worship and reverence which allows the presence of God to continually abide there.

Another benefit of having a designated place set aside for God is that not only does God know what our intentions are when we enter there, but everyone else also knows. It should be a place where family and friends do not bother you or meet you with the mundane. It is to be a quiet place, a place of prayer.

I know great men of God who have set aside entire rooms in their homes to be their secret place. Others have a corner of a room reserved for their time with God. We should give God all of the room that we can afford. If we can set a full room aside, that would be best because of the minimal distractions. However, if we can only spare a corner of a room, God will be honored by that. Ask God for His direction concerning designating a place for your time with Him and follow His instruction.

The main key of setting aside a place for God is to obey the direction of God. If God tells you that a corner of your bedroom is what He desires, give it to Him. If He asks for an addition to be built onto your house for Him, call a contractor. Nothing can be too grand for the presence of the Almighty God.

When I asked God for His direction concerning my secret place, He was very specific in His instruction. I began by informing God that I did not have any extra room in my house to set aside for our time together. He immediately responded by showing me a corner of my bedroom that was not being used. He also laid on my heart the type of furniture that I should purchase for my secret place.

The main key of setting aside a place for God is to obey His Direction.

I was concerned that my wife would not share the passion that I had for setting up a special place in our home to meet with God. I feared she would cringe at spending the money for the furniture that God had directed me to purchase. When I told my wife that I would like to look at some furniture for my secret place, she seemed almost excited. She said that God had been talking to her about the same thing.

While we were walking through the furniture store, I saw the exact chair that God had shown me in my spirit. I knew that it would be more money than we would want to spend. However, when my wife saw the same chair she exclaimed, "Jeremy, this is the one!" We decided to purchase the chair, although it was a little more expensive than we had allowed. That very week God provided more than enough money for the chair. God works in amazing ways when we follow His instructions.

Ask God for His direction concerning the secret place and follow His instruction. His presence is priceless and the ideas that He will give you in the secret place will change your life. It will be one of the greatest investments that you ever make.

Scheduled Appointment with God

One of the most powerful keys of the secret place is found in scheduling a specific time each day to meet with God. It has been a very difficult adjustment for me to make from my old casual prayer life. Too often, we attempt to "make time" to fellowship with God. We decide that we will pray when we are not as busy or when we have some extra time, however, that time of serenity never seems to come. The day comes to a close, and we retire to our bedroom without ever making time to be with Him.

Our prayer lives often are filled with quick, impromptu meetings with God. We announce our presence to Him, give Him our requests and leave.

I never realized how offensive that must have been to Him. I don't say this to be negative; I only say it to open your eyes to the fact that there is something far greater. I have found that God is very accessible and will schedule an appointment with us, whenever we are available. He desires to have long, two-way conversations with us. We must only make ourselves available to Him. When you set an appointment with God, He will be there, anxiously awaiting your arrival. When we keep our appointment with God, His presence is overwhelming because He is excited to spend time with us.

His presence is Priceless and the ideas that He will give you in the secret place will change your life.

It is extremely important to set a specific time to spend with God and keep the appointment that we have scheduled without compromise. We must understand, when we miss our scheduled time with God, it breaks His heart. We keep appointments for the mundane in our lives, but too often neglect the most important meeting of the day; our time with God.

This was something that I struggled with greatly. I would wait until I had an opportunity to pray, then I would be too tired when nighttime came. After I had not talked to God the day before, I would live in condemnation the next day. Like

Adam and Eve, I would begin to dodge the presence of God because of the condemnation I felt over not praying the day before. I allowed a small failure to turn into a much larger spiritual failure because of my guilt. This process becomes like a snowball, getting bigger by the day, until we are too ashamed and the problem seems too big to turn around. Falling prey to these emotions will cause a quick, downward spiral in your relationship with God. We must not allow the feelings of condemnation or guilt about yesterday's failure to cause us to avoid spending time with God.

> *You must never allow guilt to keep you from entering the Presence of God.*

One of the greatest changes that I have made is to ask God to forgive me when I miss my time with Him, then forgive myself for missing the greatest part of my day. <u>I believe that one of satan's biggest tricks to stop our prayer life is to cause us to feel guilt for our shortcomings rather than see the great benefits of our progress.</u> Never allow guilt over past mistakes to keep you from entering the presence of God. We must learn to put our mistakes behind us and realize that our Heavenly Father desires nothing more than to spend time with us. He is quick to forgive us in order to restore our fellowship. Nothing helps us get over the disappointments of the past like sitting in the presence of our God, who is great in mercy. If we fall off of the proverbial horse, we must get right back on and continue progressing down the path that God has in store for us.

You may be asking, *"When is the best time to make an appointment to meet God?"* The quickest and easiest answer is to meet Him each day at the same time at whatever time of the day that works best for you. Some people are morning people and would benefit the most from setting aside time early in the morning. Others are night owls and would profit most from spending the greatest portion of their time with God late at night. Others still would find the most benefit from fasting through lunch and spending their lunch hour with God. The time of day is not as crucial as the consistency with which you keep your appointment with God.

I am most certainly a night owl. My favorite time of day to work is after my children have gone to sleep. However, I find the most powerful times with God come when I crucify my flesh, get up early and spend time in prayer before the rest of my house wakes up. My personal schedule with God is to spend the biggest time of prayer early in the morning and to study my Bible at night after my kids have gone to bed and my house calms down. I struggled somewhat to find this balanced schedule. By splitting my prayer time and Bible study, I have been able to spend more time with God and my time has become more productive. My prayer time in the morning allows me to set the tone of my day by starting in the presence of God and allowing God to help me plan my day. I have found that when I allow God to help me plan my day and set my priorities that I am able to accomplish more and have a greater level of success throughout my day. However, because I am not a morning person when I try to spend all of my time with God in the mornings, I do not get as much out of my Bible study.

Doing my Bible study at night has allowed for several added benefits. First, my mind is sharper at night; therefore, my studies are more efficient then. Second, it allows me to spend more time with God than I would be able to spend in the mornings only. Third, when God is revealing a lot to me, I am able to continue my study rather than having to stop to go to work.

There is no set time or way to plan your schedule to be in the secret place. Ask God to help you find the right time to spend with Him. Listen to His voice and follow His every instruction. Obedience to God is the key to unlocking His power in your life. The only constant in all prayer lives should be acknowledging God first thing in the morning. God should be your top priority, and you should spend at least a couple of moments to greet Him in the morning and ask Him to guide you during the day.

If you are currently spending very little time with God, do not start with a goal of 1 or 2 hours per day in the secret place. Start with a goal of 5, 10, 15 or 20 minutes per day. This will allow you to start your journey with small successes. It is important to be able to build from these victories rather to try to rebound from the failures of setting a large goal that you are unable to meet. If you continue to meet your goals, raise your expectations and spend more time with God. Learn to celebrate the small victories rather than focusing on your small failures. Make your secret place a place of victory, not condemnation.

Learn to Celebrate small victories rather than focusing on your small failures.

I cannot overemphasize the importance of not living in condemnation. God will not turn away a repentant heart. He wants to restore fellowship with His children. When you miss your appointment with God, ask Him for His forgiveness and do not turn away from His presence. Learn to return as quickly as possible to the secret place and begin moving closer to God again.

Facilitates Mutual Communication

It is impossible to have an intimate relationship with God without having two-way communication with Him. In order to know God and allow Him to reveal Himself to us, we MUST allow Him to speak to us. The prayer lives of most people only allow one-way communication. God desires to have fellowship with us, and mutual communication is necessary for that to happen. The secret place facilitates mutual communication because we are in a private place with no distractions where God is our only focus.

Spending time in the secret place has allowed me to get to know God intimately because I have taken the time to listen to Him. I do not simply present my requests and move on, I spend a lot of time in worship, attentively listening for His voice. He has revealed so much of Himself to me during those times.

God loves to speak to us, and I believe the place that makes it easiest for Him do that is in the secret place. Make one of the major goals of your time in the secret place to allow God to speak to you and have true two-way communication with Him.

Allows God to Make You Who He Created You to Be

As I stated in an earlier chapter, the Holy Spirit wants to change us. He wants to give us the gifts, callings and abilities to fulfill the assignment that God has placed inside of us. When we are alone with God in the secret place the Holy Spirit has the perfect opportunity to cause us to be who He wants us to be.

Intimacy with God allows us greater access to Him and allows Him greater access to change us. In the solitude of the secret place with our heart and mind totally in tune with God, the Holy Spirit is able to speak to us and reveal things to us that will change our lives.

He has given me a whole new picture of who I am and what I am able to accomplish because of the changes that He has made in me in the secret place. I now see God's picture of me, rather than my own picture of me, and it has allowed me to step completely into the assignment which God has called me to fulfill. If I had never gone into the secret place, the Holy Spirit could not have revealed His picture of me. Therefore, I never would be able to reach the heights that God has in store because I would not have had the self-confidence to step through the doors that He has opened for me.

If we are going to reach the level that God has destined for us, we must go to the place where the Holy Spirit has jurisdiction to make the changes necessary in our lives. That place is the secret place. Meet Him there and allow Him to change you, and He will take you places that you could never imagine.

Intimacy with God allows us greater access to Him and allows Him greater access to change us.

WHAT TO DO IN THE SECRET PLACE

*T*his chapter may seem like Prayer 101 to many readers. However, I do not want anyone reading this book to commit themselves to spending time in the secret place only to find themselves lost once they get there. You may set your own agenda in the secret place, but the following is a list of things that I believe should be included in your time spent with God.

- Sing His Praises
- Pray and Seek God
- Be Quiet and Let God Talk to You
- Read and Study the Bible

Sing His Praises

The Bible is very clear that if we desire to enter into the presence with God, there is a key that unlocks His presence: sing His praises. Psalm 100:2 tells us to, *"Come before His presence with singing."* The psalmist further commands in Psalms 95:2, *"Let us come before His presence with thanksgiving; Let us shout joyfully to Him with psalms."* If we want to enter into His presence, we MUST sing. Even if you do not like to sing, you must sing if you want to experience God's presence. If you are not a good singer, you still must sing to enter His presence. Rest assured that all God is looking for is someone to make a joyful noise to Him. He is not looking for you to sound like Darlene Zscheck or Israel Houghton in order to attract His presence.

I have been obsessed with learning about the Holy Spirit while writing this book. The biggest shock I have had during this study is the fact that every teacher I have listened to about the Holy Spirit has said the biggest key to attracting the presence of God is to sing to Him. Singing to Him is extremely important. Sing His praises. Sing His Word. Sing the words that He inspires you to sing.

Enter into His Presence with singing!

Entering into His presence by singing to Him may seem unimportant and even silly, perhaps. I have felt the same way in the past. I thought that God would be far more impressed with my flowery, super-spiritual prayers. However, my theory was blown out of the water when I began singing to God, and I felt His presence rush in. When I decided to squash my pride and humble myself and sing to God, my experience with Him changed.

It may seem difficult at first, but continue singing at the beginning of your time with Him and you will feel His joy and satisfaction with your efforts.

Pray and Seek God

After you have spent time in praise and song, give God your supplications. Philippians 4:6 tells us to make our requests known to God with thanksgiving. We must learn to boldly approach God with our needs. Ask Him for direction, healing, salvation of loved ones, deliverance or whatever needs are in your life.

I have found it extremely helpful to keep a list of prayer requests in a notebook that is kept in my secret place. There are too many needs that need prayer to keep in your mind. A prayer list prevents you from forgetting any important needs.

Psalm 91:15 makes this promise to those who dwell in the secret place, *"He shall call upon Me, and I will answer him."* We cannot underestimate the power that prayer in the secret place has. We must not allow that power to go untapped. Our family, friends, leaders and co-workers need our support in prayer; it is vital that we fill that role for them. Their lives will be changed by the prayers that God hears from our secret place.

We should also seek God's direction while in our secret place. We need His constant guidance in order to remain in the center of His will. Ask Him every day to guide and direct your every step that day and to reveal His plans and assignment for your life.

I have seen a great deal of impact church services have had in my life since I began praying intently the day before services and asking God to have His way corporately and in my life individually. He has been able to do much more for me in those services because my heart was much more prepared to receive what God had in store for me.

Whatever the need may be in your life or in someone else's life, God is prepared to work on our behalf if we will ask. Ask Him with a thankful heart from your secret place and you will see God begin to do more than you could ever imagine.

Be Quiet and Let God Talk to You

This is probably the most difficult part for most people. We are really good at talking and even begging, but we are not typically very good at just listening. However, listening to God is an extremely vital part of the secret place experience.

Have you ever had someone ask you an important question and then interrupt your answer or ignore it completely because they have something more important to say? It is extremely aggravating to me when that happens. However, we do that to God all of the time. We may have a pressing need or a situation in which we need His direction, so we ask Him for an answer, only to not give Him an opportunity to answer. We either never stop talking, or we ask and leave. It is impossible for Him to help us because we do not give Him the opportunity to do His part.

Be still and listen for His Voice.

We must learn to just be still and listen for His replies to our many requests. After I have given God my concerns, questions and requests, I will begin to quietly worship and listen for His response. I have found that while I am quietly in a spirit of worship He can easily talk to me. It is that still, small voice in my spirit that gives me the answers I need. If I only ask Him for direction, then rush off to the rest of my day He will never be able to give me the idea that makes my day twice as efficient. If I ask Him for wisdom in a relationship and never stop to listen for the words He would have for me to say, that relationship may never be restored. It is imperative that we are quiet long enough for Him to respond and talk to us.

Communication should always be a two-way conversation. All too often our prayers are a soliloquy outlining our concerns and complaints. We must allow our prayer life to become a two way communication where God can talk back to us and change our lives.

Read and Study the Bible

Reading and studying the Bible in the secret place should be more than attempting to log chapters and "get through it". Always begin your Bible study with prayer asking God to open your eyes to the truths that He has for you in the Bible. Ask Him to help you to retain what you read and give you supernatural understanding.

Never allow your Bible study to become merely about reading a certain number of chapters in order to keep you from feeling guilty. Prayerfully read your Bible and strive to understand its application to your life.

There are several approaches to daily Bible reading. You can read slowly and study each scripture as you go, or you can read more quickly in order to read through the entire Bible. I believe that we should make an attempt to do each of these regularly. My normal routine consists of both deep study of a certain book or topic and reading more quickly a certain block of chapters. By using this approach I am able to frequently read through the Bible as well as getting deeper revelation on topics that I am studying.

When I am doing my quicker reading, I frequently find scriptures that I would like to study further. I have a section in my notebook for writing the scripture reference and any short notes that sparked my interest in that passage. Before I began noting scriptures for further study, I frequently got bogged down in a passage, studying as I went, and was unable to read through the Bible in a reasonable time frame.

It is important to find a Bible study routine that fits your Bible reading goals and individual needs. If you struggle with finding a routine you are comfortable with, ask God for help or consult a spiritual mentor for guidance. The most important thing is not the regimen you use, but that you daily read from the Word of God and allow God to speak to you through His Word.

You may find other things that you like to do in your secret place, but these four things should be a staple in your time with God each day. Allow God to continue to direct you and keep your time with Him fresh and dynamic.

WHAT TO KEEP IN THE SECRET PLACE

*T*his chapter is designed for two main purposes. The first purpose is to help make your time in the secret place as effective and efficient as possible, and secondly to help you prevent some of the pitfalls that satan will throw your way to stop your time with God.

Preparing your secret place can be the key to success for your time of fellowship with God. Your secret place needs to have an atmosphere of worship and expectancy so that you can readily enter the presence of God. Prepare the area with that goal. Some people like to have candles lit, others like dim lights, and others like to have plentiful sunshine. The most important thing is not the light level, but the atmosphere of the room.

In order for your secret place to be effective and efficient, you should have certain items available. First and foremost you should have a Bible. Many times God speaks to us through His Word, so we should keep it close in our secret place. Second, you should have a prayer journal to keep prayer requests and praise reports. Having a list of prayer requests helps you remember to pray for those in need. Suggestions for your prayer list would include: family members, friends who need God's direction, people with illnesses, unsaved loved ones, Pastors, Evangelists, Missionaries, small group leaders, government leaders, and many, many more. You can have a written list of needs, or you can have pictures of those you regularly pray for in an album or hanging on the wall.

You also should have a journal in which you can write the revelations God gives you. God will not continue to give you revelation if you have no way to document or remember it. *Honor His revelation enough to Write it Down.* God has told me many things that were so extraordinary and amazing that I was sure I would never forget them. Later, I would sit down to write them in a journal I would not remember what God had told me. You may be thinking, "Why would God allow you to forget?" The answer is that I did not honor His revelation enough to get a pen and paper to write down the life-changing epiphany. God will reveal much more to us if we will document what He tells us.

Digital voice recorders are a great way to record songs or revelation that God gives you in the secret place. They are fairly inexpensive, but I believe they are indispensable. When I am praying,

God often speaks to me, and I do not want to have to take the time to write what He has told me. Now that I have a voice recorder, I simply record His message and continue praying. I am able to replay and transfer the information to a journal or computer at a later time.

Playing worship music really fosters an atmosphere of praise and ushers in the presence of God. I like to keep a MP3 player in my secret place, so I can play selected songs during my time with God. You may choose to use a CD player or some other type of media player, but it is important to have music playing that creates an atmosphere of praise, without the distractions of commercials. I have a separate playlist on my MP3 player, specifically for use in the secret place.

When you make the decision to spend time in the secret place developing an intimate relationship with God, satan will do everything he can to distract you and cause you to leave that place of closeness with God. Therefore, you must learn his schemes and prevent their effectiveness against you. One of his main tricks is to remind you of things that you should be doing instead of spending time with God. You can counteract this by keeping a notebook handy to write down things he reminds you that you have forgotten, so you can do them when you are finished.

What to Keep in The Secret Place

If you feel like you need to cut your time short because you are thirsty, keep a glass of water in your secret place. If hunger always seems to strike in the middle of your time in the secret place, keep some crackers handy. Whatever satan uses to distract you, find a way to prevent that from causing you to cut your time short with God.

My biggest problem is that I am not a morning person at all; however, I like to pray first thing in the morning. If I attempt to go straight from bed to the secret place, inevitably I will get extremely tired, if not fall asleep. Falling asleep while you are praying in the secret place causes you to feel extremely unholy and condemned. I try to avoid that at all costs. My remedy to being tired when I pray is to get up, eat breakfast and move around a little before I go into my secret place. By making this one change, my time of prayer in the morning is much longer, enjoyable and more powerful.

Satan will do whatever he can to cut short our time with God. We must learn his strategies and keep them from being effective against us.

As you spend more time in the secret place you will find things that you like to have with you and will create your own atmosphere and routine. Allow God to guide you and follow His direction to make your secret place a place of nearness to God.

BENEFITS OF THE SECRET PLACE

There are many benefits of spending time with the Almighty in the Secret Place. Spending time with God in the Secret Place is its own reward; however, in keeping with God's character He makes sure that we receive many more blessings. *It is impossible to give to God without receiving much more in return.* When we give our time and attention to God, He blesses us in many different ways. This chapter will outline 21 of the benefits that come from dwelling in the Secret Place.

Increased Productivity

"I don't have any extra time to spend in the secret place!" Does this sound familiar? It is a popular refrain when Christians are challenged to begin spending time with God in the secret place. Every time I have made that challenge, somebody will respond they don't have the time to spare. It is a fact that in our culture we have more things to do than we have time to do them. Many use this as a reason to skip their time with God. However, I would submit that being extremely busy is the best reason TO SPEND time with God. When we give anything to God, it is His nature to bountifully re-

turn it back to us. The Bible is very clear in Galatians 6:8 that we will reap whatever we sow. If we give time to God, He WILL give us much more time in return. If you find yourself in a position where you do not think you have time to get everything done, that is when it is most important for you to give time to God. It may sound a little crazy to give more of your time to God, when you seem to have the least amount to spare, but when you place God first and sacrificially give time to Him, He will increase your productivity. I have found that God will give you ideas to increase your effectiveness, help you better plan your time, and remove obstacles in order to make you more productive.

> *It is Impossible to give to God without receiving much more in return.*

Proverbs 3:2 states if you follow God's commands that length of days AND long life will be added to you. God is the great steward and He was not just trying to increase the word count of Proverbs. He meant that not only would He give you a longer life, but He would also make your days "longer" or more productive. In other words, because of Him you are able to fit more work into a day than someone who does not follow His commands. If we give time to God in the secret place He will multiply our time back to us by giving us length of days and increased productivity.

Stress Relief

Spending time with God is a great way to relieve stress. It is far better than squeezing a ball, throwing a tantrum or kicking a dog. If you have trouble managing your stress, I can give you no greater advice than to "unwind" in the presence of God. God will listen to your problems and your cares and lighten your load. 1 Peter 5:7 says, "cast all your cares upon Him for He cares for you." Think about that for a moment. God is asking you to cast ALL your cares on Him. He strongly desires to be the one you go to with all the problems in your life because He cares so deeply about us.

There have been many times I have allowed stress to dominate my mind. When stress would come, I would begin allowing my thoughts to spiral downhill until all I could think about was the set of circumstances that caused my anxiety. However, after I discovered the secret place, I began spending time with God when I was stressed out. I found it to the most relaxing and healing thing I could possibly do to stop the downward spiral and get back on the right track. Now when stress or anxiety attacks, the first thing I do is head to my secret place and cast my cares upon God and allow Him to bring peace back into my heart.

It is easy to get stressed out and full of anxiety, but always remember where you can find a respite *from the rigors of life. Acts 3:19 reminds us "Times of refreshing may come from the presence of the Lord."* Circumstances of life have the ability to cause our souls to dry out. They can sap all of our joy and peace. Our spirit can become parched. It is in those times that we must go to the secret place and enter the presence of the Lord and allow Him to refresh our souls. Like a spring in the middle of the desert, God can refresh us at the time we need it the most. Spending time with God in the secret place is the best stress relief you will ever find.

Revelation

I once heard a well-known preacher say, "God will tell you things in the secret place that no one else can tell you." Immediately, my spirit leapt within me. I realized that one of the greatest changes in my relationship with God, since I had begun my practice of spending time in the secret place, was an increase in revelation from God. Scriptures from the Bible seemingly jumped off of the page during my Bible study. As I read the Bible, I would feel God's emotions and receive supernatural insight into the deeper meaning of the scriptures. However, my increase in revelation has gone further than Biblical insight. God has given me revelation on work-related issues, relationships, and finances. When we separate ourselves from the distractions of the world and focus all our attention on God, He will respond by giving us revelation concerning the most important issues in our lives.

God is able to tell us things in the secret place that He would normally be unable to tell us any other time because there is a higher level of intimacy and focus. I noticed an increase in revelation from God very quickly. Much of the revelation for this book was given to me in one hour in a hotel room the afternoon I discovered the secret place. God showed me the difference between the secret place versus a casual prayer life, how it affects our relationship with Him, the benefits of spending time in the secret place and what the secret place was not.  The revelation just exploded in my heart, and I took notes as hard and fast as I could in order to document everything He was revealing. It was most certainly one of the greatest turning points in my life.

Something special happens when we shut out the rest of the world and purposefully spend time in communication with God that unlocks the door of His revelation.

Joy

> *In Your presence is fullness of joy;*
> *At Your right hand*
> *are pleasures forevermore.*
> Psalms 16:11

God has given us His presence for our joy. We look to many different things to provide us joy. However, when we look somewhere other than to God, we are always left wanting. Fullness of joy is found in the presence of God. David realized this fact. He had everything in life that should make a man happy. He had power, fame, prestige and money; but he says that the greatest joy comes from spending time in the presence of God. The same holds true for us today. When life steals our joy, we can look in many places for something to restore our joy back to us, but only one thing will truly satisfy.

I learned to rely on the presence of God for my joy when I read and decided to commit to memory the following scripture.

> *You have made him exceedingly glad*
> *with Your presence.*
> Psalms 21:6

After I memorized this verse, anytime my joy was lost, I would make this my prayer, "You have made me <u>exceedingly glad</u> with Your presence." Quickly, God overflows me with His presence and joy. No matter what life throws my way, as long as I can go into His presence my joy can always be sustained, because He has given me His presence for my joy.

Marriages Are Healed

As I was preparing a new series for the young adult group that I was leading, I seriously considered starting a series on marriage. God quickened my spirit to teach on the secret place instead. I questioned Him because I knew some of the couples in my group were struggling in their marriages. God told me if they would begin to spend time in the secret place and draw closer to Him, He would be able to change them, and by changing them, heal their marriage.

When we develop an intimate relationship with God, He can change our marriage by changing the way we see our spouse. When we see our spouse as a gift from God, meant to be the object of our love and affection, it is more difficult to verbally abuse them than it is when we view them as our maid or meal ticket.

Another way that God can change our marriage through a deeper relationship with Him is by changing the way we approach problems in our marriages. When counseling couples you typically spend a majority of the time hearing one person talking about what the other is doing wrong. Individuals in marriage counseling rarely say what they are doing incorrectly. However, God changed that dramatically for me in the secret place. I have noticed that when I complain to God about what my wife is doing wrong, He never tells me what she needs to do to fix our problem. He always tells me what I need to do to fix it. While it is aggravating at the time, this has been remarkable for my marriage.

If your marriage is struggling, grow closer to God, spend time talking to Him in the secret place and follow His instructions. He is able to heal even the most broken marriages.

Divine Protection

> *1 He who dwells in the secret place of the Most High Shall abide under the shadow of the Almighty. 2 I will say of the LORD, "He is my refuge and my fortress; My God, in Him I will trust." 3 Surely He shall deliver you from the snare of the fowler And from the perilous pestilence. 4 He shall cover you with His feathers, And under His wings you shall*

take refuge; His truth shall be your shield and buckler.
9 Because you have made the LORD, who is my refuge, Even the Most High, your dwelling place, 10 No evil shall befall you, Nor shall any plague come near your dwelling; 11 For He shall give His angels charge over you, To keep you in all your ways. 12 In their hands they shall bear you up, Lest you dash your foot against a stone.
Psalms 91:1-4, 9-12

    God promises protection to those who dwell in His secret place. Psalms 91 is a beautiful reminder of God's protection for us. God loves to spend time with His children, and He will take care of those who reciprocate that feeling. It is easy to feel God's enthusiasm in this passage of scripture. He says that because we make Him our dwelling place that He will divinely protect us from evil even to the point where He gives angels charge over us to protect us. If God has this kind of exhilaration when we spend time with Him, how can we ignore His gentle bidding in order to watch a few more minutes of television? He loves to spend time with us and one of the ways He shows His appreciation for us is by divinely protecting us from the snares of the enemy.

You shall hide them in
the secret place of Your presence
From the plots of man;
You shall keep them secretly in a pavilion
From the strife of tongues.
Psalms 31:20

Guidance

As we already discussed, God will tell you things in the secret place that no one else can tell you. Christians should never make any major decisions without looking for the guidance of the Holy Spirit in the secret place. The Holy Spirit is a phenomenal mentor, and we should constantly seek His guidance. *The Holy Spirit is a phenomenal mentor.* The Holy Spirit can guide you at all times and in any place. However, it is much easier to receive His guidance in the solitude of the secret place.

God cares deeply about every aspect of our lives. He is not only concerned about our spiritual lives or ministry, but about all areas. He cares about our jobs, our relationships and even our recreation. Allow Him access into every area of your life and ask Him for His guidance in all of your decisions. Proverbs 3:5, 6 instructs, *"Trust the Lord with all your heart, and lean not on YOUR OWN understanding. In ALL your ways acknowledge Him; And He shall direct your paths."* It is difficult to lean on God's guidance rather than your own understanding. It is a process that happens over time as you trust God and follow Him rather than acting out your own plan. You quickly learn that God's ways truly are higher than our ways and that things turn out far better when we act out His plan rather than our own. I can assure you if you give God a chance to guide you through one decision, you will learn that He is worthy of your trust. After you have learned you can trust His guidance, the next step is to turn EVERY thing over to Him like Proverbs 3:6 instructs. All too often, we put God in a box and assume that He is only involved in spiritual matters. Turn every decision over to Him. He will direct your paths in every area of your life. The path on which God directs, leads to life, joy, prosperity and victory in our lives.

When you are in your secret place, ask God for guidance in ALL areas of your life, follow His instructions and watch your life turn around as you allow the greatest mentor to direct your life and lead you to the victorious life you desire.

Rewarded by God

The Bible teaches us that when we pray in secret that God will reward us openly in Matthew 6:6, 18. God is not looking for people who only pray in public in order to get noticed by others. He is looking for those who pray to Him because they take delight in spending time with Him, therefore, He promises to reward openly those who pray to Him in secret.

God is simply looking for excuses to bless us and show Himself to be faithful to those around us. Give Him a chance to reward you by spending time with Him in the secret place and watch what He begins to do in your life.

Psalms 37:4 says, *"Delight yourself in the Lord, and He will give you the desires of your heart."* God also talks about the rewards He has in store for us in Psalms 91:14-16.

When we spend time with God in the secret place demonstrating our love and desire to be with Him, He will reward us and show off in front of the world on our behalf.

Assignments Are Revealed

God has given to each and every person an assignment. We are all called to be ministers in some capacity. The ministry to which we are called is our God-given assignment. Much of the frustration in our lives can be traced to doing things outside of our assignment and failing to do the things we are called to do. It is vitally important for us, as Christians, to discover our assignment that God has given to us to be fulfilled on the earth.

God specifically told me He reveals our assignment in the secret place. It is easy to mistake our personal wants and desires to be the voice of God calling us to that thing we desire. Therefore, it is vitally important that we go to the secret place; spend time alone with God, seeking His face specifically concerning your assignment. When we are in the presence of God, totally focused on Him, it is much easier to hear and discern His voice and His calling.

Visions Are Birthed

In addition to our assignments being revealed in the secret place, God will very often draw us into a solitary place to birth new visions into our spirit. When God has a new plan for His people, it is birthed as a vision in the heart of one of His people. People across the world would not be reached for Christ without missionaries having visions seeing the unchurched throngs saved in the villages of remote areas across the globe. God gives His people pictures of what is possible if they follow His directions. These visions are the driving force of the burning desire to do what has never been done before.

Before you can do the unimaginable in the public place, you must first get a picture of it in the secret place. Rinehard Bonnke is one of the greatest evangelists the world has ever seen. Under his ministry many, many millions of people have been saved. Before that great ministry ever came to fruition, during his time of prayer, he received a vision from God of "the entire continent of Africa, covered in the precious blood of Jesus." Before he was the world renowned soul winner that he is today, he was a man with a vision from God.

If we are to accomplish the great and mighty things that God has in store for each and every one of us, we must discover our assignment and receive the vision that will ignite a flame inside of us to carry us through the storms that will come against us as we follow the plan of God. Hang on to the picture God has placed in your heart in the secret place and pursue it with everything within you. Then it is possible to begin accomplishing things you would have never dreamt possible.

Fulfillment

We seem to look for fulfillment everywhere in our lives. We look for a mate to fulfill us. We look for a better job that we believe will fulfill us. We decide to have children thinking that will fulfill us. Others look to alcohol or drugs for their fulfillment. It seems as though everyone is always looking for something to "complete" them.

We put undue pressure on those closest to us to make us happy and make us feel complete. Many marriages fall apart because each spouse is expecting the other to do whatever it takes to make them happy. I experienced this early in my marriage. In order for me to be happy, I needed my wife to go above and beyond the call of duty to make sure that all of my needs and wants were met. I do not believe that I am the only person who has ever had those expectations. No matter how wonderful your spouse may be they can never take the place of God in your life. If you expect any human to fulfill you, it will only lead to failure and disappointment.

As I began spending time in the secret place and developing a more intimate relationship with God, I realized that the only way I could possibly be fulfilled is by being closer to Him. I looked everywhere for my fulfillment, but the only true fulfillment comes from God. As long as you look in other places for fulfillment, you will always be left disappointed. You must look only to God to fill the void inside you.

A great benefit to spending time in the secret place was finding my fulfillment in God. I no longer need the approval of others, the excessive effort of my wife, constant accolades of man or anything else of this world to make me feel complete. I have found my fulfillment in the Friend that sticks closer than a brother, my Heavenly Father and my constant Guide and Companion, the Holy Spirit. The only true fulfillment comes from Him.

Get Strength to Overcome

When circumstances come against you, and you need the strength of God in order to rise above them and overcome, go to the secret place. 1 Corinthians 16:27 tells us strength is in His place. When you need strength, go to His place. You will find God and His strength to overcome there.

Spiritual Rest

Running from place to place...stress from work...trying to keep everyone around you satisfied...hustle and bustle every day. Does this sound familiar?

It is easy to be swallowed up by life. You end up exhausted and emotionally drained. Everywhere you turn you hear the same things from seemingly everyone. They say it is the American way and there is no way around it; you just have to learn to cope with it.

There is an answer to the exhaustion and emotional emptiness that you feel.

It is found in Matthew 11:28, where God promises, *"Come to Me...I will give you rest."* Come to God, draw near to Him, and you will find the rest for which you have been longing. God does not want His people to be wore down and battered by life. He wants us to be full of peace from the rest that we have found in Him. If you are trying to find a respite from the rigors of life, you will find it when you spend time with the Prince of Peace in the secret place.

Find a respite for the rigors of life by cultivating your relationship with the Prince of Peace

Greater Evangelistic Fire

One of the most surprising benefits I have found from spending time in the secret place is a greater desire to win the lost for Christ. The more time I spent with God, the more I learned about Him. The more I learned about Him, the more I loved Him. The more I loved Him, the more I wanted every person in the world to know Him. I never expected to have my evangelistic fire stoked in the secret place, but God certainly adds fuel each time I spend quiet time with Him.

Wisdom Is Imparted

"If any of you lacks wisdom, let him ask of God, who gives to all liberally and without reproach, and it will be given to him."
James 1:5

As I prayed in the secret place this morning, God laid a certain subject on my heart, and I realized that I needed wisdom in that area. I prayed specifically that God would grant me wisdom for that need. Immediately, as I prayed, the Holy Spirit directed me to get my notebook and begin writing a series of questions on that topic. After I had finished, He directed me to call a mentor He had placed in my life and ask the questions He had given me.

I have found that God will give us wisdom when we ask. However, He rarely will simply lay out the information we need directly in front of us. He gives us instructions. He brings a person into our life that can grant wisdom in that area. He works in many ways that we do not always acknowledge; however, He still is at work. Such was the case during my quiet time this morning. God showed me an area in which I would need wisdom in the immediate future and laid out the blueprint for acquiring the information I would need.

Make it a habit to ask God for wisdom in your secret place. Whether you know you are about to face a situation where you will need His wisdom, or you just desire wisdom in any area He deems necessary, always ask for wisdom. It is one of the major keys to living a successful, joy-filled life.

As Proverbs 4:7 teaches, *"Wisdom is the principal thing, therefore, get wisdom; and in all your getting, get understanding."* So always strive for wisdom and allow God to bless you with abundant wisdom as you spend time with Him in the secret place.

Increased Effectiveness of Prayer

"Because he has set his love upon Me, therefore I will deliver him; I will set him on high, because he has known My name. He shall call upon Me, and I will answer him."
Psalm 91:14, 15

Dwelling with God in the secret place brings greater effectiveness to your prayers. There are a couple reasons that cause this to be true. First, when you spend a lot of time in the secret place you are more in tune with the heart of God and are more receptive to His voice. Therefore, your prayers reflect the will of God much more than the selfish prayers that come from a more casual prayer life.

The second reason is God loves to spend time in fellowship with us. He says in Psalm 91:15 He will answer us when we call on Him, if we set our love upon Him and dwell in the secret place with Him. He has an insatiable desire to spend time with us; therefore, He is a faithful rewarder of those who reciprocate that desire back to Him.

Spending time in the secret place with God changes our hearts, our desires and also our relationship with God. The end result of that change is a more effective prayer life.

DWELLING WITH GOD in the Secret Place brings greater effectiveness to your prayers.

Used More by the Holy Spirit

As I have stated multiple times in earlier chapters, our relationship with God changes as we develop a more intimate relationship with Him. A side effect of that change that I have noticed in my life is an ability to be used more often and more powerfully by the Holy Spirit. As I become closer and closer to God, growing more familiar with His voice and more eager to follow His instructions, the Holy Spirit is able to use me in more situations than He was able to use me in before.

He uses me to reach people in church services, in counseling sessions and most often in normal conversation. During normal conversations God will give me wisdom to share. Many times people have told me they have been praying about that subject and our conversation was an answer to prayer. There was no big build up, no "Thus sayeth the Lord", no sounding of trumpets, just the Holy Spirit working through me because I am attentive to His voice.

I say all of that not to brag on me, but to brag on what God is able to do when we focus our lives on Him.

The same is possible for everyone. We can all reach so many more people; even those who are seemingly unwilling to listen to the Word of God. God can reach them through a subtle, Spirit-led comment when the greatest evangelist in the world would have no chance to reach them by conventional means. If you want to be used more mightily by the Holy Spirit, draw closer to God by spending time with Him in the secret place, learning to recognize His voice and follow His instructions.

> IT'S AMAZING what God can do when we Focus our lives on Him.

Deliverance From Fear

*"He shall cover you with His feathers, And under His wings you shall take refuge; His truth shall be your shield and buckler. **You shall not be afraid** of the terror by night, Nor of the arrow that flies by day, Nor of the pestilence that walks in darkness, Nor of the destruction that lays waste at noonday."*
Psalm 91:4-6

The person who dwells in the secret place will be delivered from fear. When fear grips your life, you can be totally derailed from the plans that God has for you. Do not give in to fear, but combat it by spending time in the presence of God. Bask in His love because "Perfect love casts out all fear."

Deliverance In Times of Trouble

"Because he has set his love upon Me, therefore I will deliver him; I will set him on high, because he has known My name. He shall call upon Me, and I will answer him; I will be with him in trouble; I will deliver him and honor him. With long life I will satisfy him, And show him My salvation." Psalm 91:14-16

God makes the promise in Psalm 91, He will deliver those who dwell with Him from times of trouble. John 16:33 informs us, we will have trouble, but that God will overcome them all.

We see this illustrated in the life of Daniel. Because Daniel prayed to God, he was thrown into a den of lions. Obviously, this was a time of severe trouble. There seemed to be no way out for Daniel. However, the Bible teaches Daniel prayed three times each day to God and God was there to deliver Daniel from his time of trouble. He shut the mouths of the lions and brought Daniel through his brush with death. Daniel was faithful in spending time in prayer to God and God was faithful to Daniel when he was in a time of trouble.

The same will hold true for us today. If we remain faithful to God, He will be faithful to see us through our times of trials.

Intimacy With God

There is one benefit that far outweighs all the others for me. By spending time in the secret place, I have cultivated a more intimate relationship with God than I ever could have imagined. Due to this intimacy, God has revealed so much about Himself to me. I have learned so much about His personality and His feelings toward me. As I learn more about God and the more I know Him, the more I love Him.

Having an intimate relationship with God is similar to a relationship with your spouse. It is impossible to have a strong relationship without spending time together or just talking when you have the time. You must make your husband or wife a high priority and give them your time even when other things are clamoring for your attention. When you give them time that costs you something, they realize that you place a high value on them. Your relationship grows stronger because of the closeness that comes from spending precious time together.

God is Passionate about spending time with us!

The same holds true for your relationship with God. If you only give God the time that you have left over after all of your other tasks are done, it is impossible to develop an intimate relationship with God.

I have never understood why God so fervently desires to have a relationship with me, but the more I get to know Him the stronger I feel His passion. I am extremely humbled every time I think about how much the God of all creation wants to spend time with someone like me. Even as I write, I am moved at this thought.

He desires the same type of relationship with everyone who reads this book. The reason spending time with Him in the secret place is so important, is so we can develop a closer, more intimate relationship with God. *James 4:8 promises, "Draw near to God, and He will draw near to you."* Start spending time with God in the solitude of the secret place and let Him know the greatest desire of your heart is to know Him more and become closer to Him. God will be faithful to draw near to you and reveal Himself in ways that you could never imagine. That kind of relationship with God is the prize of life.

Victorious Life

"A thousand may fall at your side, And ten thousand at your right hand; But it shall not come near you. You shall tread upon the lion and the cobra, The young lion and the serpent you shall trample underfoot." Psalm 91:7, 13

Every person in the world desires to live a victorious life exhibited by overcoming the inevitable obstacles that come against them. That desire can be fulfilled by learning to dwell in the secret place under the shadow of the Almighty. Psalm 91 talks about the kind of life that I yearn to have. If you, too, desire that type of overcoming, victorious life; you must only follow one simple instruction. Dwell with God. It is not a complicated equation, but it is definitely powerful.

I long for my life to be defined by an intimate relationship with God because that lifestyle rises above all of the tragedies and aggravations that life has to offer. That is the key to a victorious life. Closeness to God equals separation from the world and all of the negative things that accompany it.

If your lifestyle does not scream, "VICTORY!!!" right now; MAKE A CHANGE! Draw nearer to God and further from the world. Victory will most definitely be the result.

Closeness to God is the key to a VICTORIOUS LIFE.

YOU CAN KNOW HIM!

The entire basis for this book is to guide you into a more intimate relationship with God. He greatly desires to spend time with you. Whether you have never asked Christ into your heart, have your Doctorate of Divinity from seminary or are somewhere between, He wants to be with YOU! He wants to reveal Himself to you and cultivate a close, passionate relationship with you.

I began the book with a simple question. *"Are you as close to God as you want to be?"* You can get as close as you want, but it does not happen automatically. You have to reach. The reward far outweighs the costs. The greatest times of my life have come in the presence of God. There is no place like being in His presence. Nothing matches feeling His arms of love when we need comfort or the sense that His arm of strength is protecting us in time of trouble.

If you are not sure you are as close to God as you would like to be, there is a simple solution. Make a commitment to spend some time with God each day. As I said earlier, don't set unreachable goals. Start small and win small battles. Work your way up from there. Ask God for His direction on the place and time for your secret place. If you mess up, don't quit. Ask forgiveness and move onward and upward. Don't let satan win that battle.

Do you want to continue with life as usual or do you want to make time in your hectic schedule to spend time with God in the secret place? The result of that decision determines your future. You can continue the struggles that have plagued you in the past, or you can unlock the power of the presence of God and watch as your life is radically changed.

It may seem odd that God wants to be with us, but He does. Will you answer His call? Will you pledge to make spending time with God your top priority? Or will you leave Him waiting on you? The decision is yours. We can know Him: His joys, His pains, His pleasures, His frustrations. All we have to do is draw near to Him and He will draw near to us.

ACKNOWLEDGEMENTS

There are so many people who have made this book possible. Thank you to everyone who helped me to do what I believed was unthinkable. When God led me to write The Secret Place, I felt extremely unqualified and incapable. However, God quickly showed me that He was in control and put wonderful people around me to help make this dream a reality.

My biggest thank you is reserved for God. He led me by the hand as I went through this process. Getting to know Him is the greatest achievement of my life. I hope this book inspires people to know Him the way I have grown to know Him. Without an intimate relationship with God, life would have no fulfillment.

To God--Thank You for sending your Son to die on the cross for my sins. Because of that sacrifice, I have been given an abundant life and will be able to reign with you for eternity in Heaven.

To my wife, Charity--Thank you for the countless hours of proofreading, design and formatting that you have invested into this book. You have been a great source of support as I have endeavored to complete this book. You will never know what it means to me to have such a big fan.

To my parents--Thank you for your insight, opinions and prayers. You have believed in my abilities, and I have gained tremendous strength from that belief.

To my sister--Thank you for all of your English prowess. I needed a "comma cop" and someone to put a red mark through all of my "that"s. Thank you for serving that role. My book would have been a grammatical mess without your guidance.

To everyone who prayed and gave me advice throughout this process, I give a great, big "THANK YOU". I will never forget all of the help I was given.